CW00404801

SPIRIT OF
MANCHESTER

MIKE HEATH

First published in Great Britain in 2009

British Library Cataloguing-in-Publication Data
A CIP record for this title is available from the British Library

ISBN 978 1 906887 34 6

PiXZ Books
Halsgrove House, Ryelands Industrial Estate,
Bagley Road, Wellington, Somerset TA21 9PZ
Tel: 01823 653777
Fax: 01823 216796
email: sales@halsgrove.com

An imprint of Halstar Ltd, part of the Halsgrove group of companies.
Information on all Halsgrove titles is available at: www.halsgrove.com

Printed and bound by Grafiche Flaminia, Italy

Introduction

The City of Manchester is regarded by many as the world's first industrial city and where the industrial revolution began. Today many of the trademark Victorian buildings still stand and much of the canal, road and rail infrastructure built during the nineteenth century remains. However, Manchester has always had the ability to embrace change throughout its history and in recent years has undergone much development and regeneration. New public spaces have been created around modern, imaginative buildings, with their cutting-edge architecture set side by side with fine examples of the more traditional Victorian buildings, many of which have themselves been internally transformed to meet the needs of today's Mancunians. In fact it is the imaginative thinking on the refurbishment of old and often derelict buildings that sets Manchester apart.

But buildings are just a small part of what is now one of the most dynamic cities in Europe. Year on year there is an ever-growing programme of events and festivals held in and around the city centre attracting visitors from all corners of the world to say nothing of the cream of international graduates attracted to the first class university.

For my first non-railway title for Halsgrove, I became nocturnal, recording this vibrant city 'after dark' for the book *Manchester Illuminated* which was published in June 2009.

The images in that book depicted the city's shiny new structures, rejuvenated buildings from a bygone era and numerous events that combined have created one of England's great cities – all viewed from a nocturnal perspective. Now, released from the 'night-shift', I have retraced my steps during predominantly daylight hours to produce this pocket format book, a fitting souvenir of this exciting and lively city.

Mike Heath July 2009

The Manchester skyline.
A telephoto shot taken
from the viewing gallery
of the Imperial War Museum
at Salford Quays.

5

Remnants of the city's earliest settlement, the Roman Fort at Castlefield, are overshadowed by Beetham Tower, a recent residential development which includes the Hilton Hotel and is the tallest building in the North West.

(This page and overleaf)
Panoramic nightscapes
are available to customers
of the Cloud 23 Bar
and Restaurant on the 23rd
floor of the Hilton Hotel.

The Castlefield area, Britain's first Urban Heritage Park, encompasses much of Manchester's industrial heritage with its Victorian railway viaducts criss-crossing the canal systems.

In the midst of all the Victorian splendour is the 'new' Merchants Bridge.
This tubular steel structure was erected in 1996.

The area also boasts one of the world's oldest railway stations, Liverpool Road Station. This now forms part of the Manchester Museum of Science and Industry where the workshops have constructed 'Planet', a fully operational replica of the first locomotive on the Liverpool to Manchester line.

Victoria Station, once one of the largest passenger railway stations in the world. The Edwardian frontage retains the ornate iron and glass canopy bearing the names of original destinations served by the Lancashire & Yorkshire Railway.

Piccadilly Station, the first taste of the city for those arriving by train, was remodelled for the 2002 Commonwealth Games.

On the approach to the station is Gateway House. An imposing serpentine office block which dates from the 1960s and replaced old railway warehouses. It is perhaps no surprise to learn that it is nicknamed 'the lazy S'.

The Metrolink tramway passes through the city centre
streets linking the two major railway stations.

Opposite: Manchester Cathedral. Much of what is seen today
dates from the nineteenth century restoration, although parts
of the tower base date back to 1380.

Across Cathedral Gardens buildings spanning many centuries stand side by side.
The Triangle is a reincarnation of an old beloved building. This former
Corn Exchange is now a shopping centre housing famous high street outlets.

The angular-shaped building with its massive glass façade is Urbis.
This museum of urban life was opened in 2002.

The Printworks is one of the most innovative entertainment centres in the North West. This leisure complex is housed in a former printing works and the façade is more than a century old.

On the other side of the Triangle is Exchange Square the location of the Manchester Wheel which despite its size is not a permanent structure. It is however a wonderful subject for photography, especially after dark.

The redevelopment after the terrorist bomb of 1996 included the dismantling and relocation, just off Exchange Square, of the Old Wellington Inn and Sinclair's Oyster Bar

In May 2008 the square was taken over by Glasgow Rangers fans who had migrated south to support their team in the final of the U.E.F.A. Cup. The game was played at the City of Manchester Stadium and was one of the biggest sporting events hosted by the city since the 2002 Commonwealth Games.

The City of Manchester Stadium, since renamed Eastlands, is now the home of the 'Blues'.

Across the city is Old Trafford, home of the 'Red Devils'.

Opposite:
There are many sporting activities in the city's events' calendar. The annual Manchester 10K run is well supported as thousands line the streets to shout encouragement…

Right:
…to all participants be they serious athletes or not!!

The previous photographs were taken at the junction of Deansgate and Whitworth Street. Viewed from above Manchester's transport network is seen in all its forms.

Those seeking retail therapy
are spoilt for choice.

The Arndale is one of Europe's largest enclosed shopping centres.

King Street is lined with some of Manchester's most exclusive shops and leads to the city's financial district with its imposing former banking buildings.

Barton Arcade is a nineteenth century version of the Arndale. Located between Deansgate and St Ann's Square, this cast iron and glass structure has been rightly listed as a building of special architectural interest.

St Ann's Square itself is a very pleasant and spacious area to shop, meet or just sit and relax.

All round the city,
shoppers and tourists
can pause to be
entertained by
street performers...

…or marvel at the skills of local artists.

The view down lower Market Street and another contrast in architecture.
On the left is the Royal Exchange building formerly the historic Cotton Exchange.
To the right is the recently rebuilt flagship Marks & Spencer store.

What do you do with an old historic building that has outlived its original function? The Royal Exchange Theatre is a futuristic hi-tech structure, clad in metal and glass, and sited within the Great Hall of the old Cotton Exchange building. Ingenuity at its finest!

Spinningfields is a newly developed quarter combining retail,
leisure, business and public open spaces.

Opposite: It is a very peaceful location and just a short distance from the city centre.

Peter Street displays architecture to suit all tastes. The Great Northern
Railway Company's Warehouse dominates the junction with Deansgate.

The square fronting the warehouse hosts several cafés and bars.

A little nearer St Peter's Square is Manchester's most famous building,
The Free Trade Hall (right) with its Italian-influenced frontage alongside
the city's oldest theatre, the Theatre Royale which dates from 1845
and is now a night club.

Next comes St George's House which was built in 1911 for the Y.M.C.A. Its brown and buff Burmantoft terracotta façade is similar in style to the Y.M.C.A. in Brooklyn, New York which dates from 1885. Manchester's greatest hotel, the Midland Hotel, completes the line-up.

Built by the Midland Railway Company between 1898 and 1903 this immense Renaissance-style block clad in red brick, polished granite and pink and brown terracotta is best known as the place where Mr Rolls first met Mr Royce. Their world-famous car company was formed in 1906.

Piccadilly Gardens is an oasis of greenery and water in the heart of the shopping district.

This open space is an ideal venue for events like The Northern Quarter Festival –
'Hungry Pigeon' – which in 2009 aimed to put the spotlight on creative artists
both local and from across the UK.

On hot summer days the fountains provide endless fun for children of all ages.

Throughout the year festivals are held around the city. Over the Bank Holiday weekend at the beginning of May 2009 Mancunians had the opportunity to sample a slice of Mediterranean life in the heart of the city. Many of the events took place in a giant Perspex pavilion that was erected in Albert Square in front of the town hall.

A popular attraction was the dressage from Minorca with highly trained riders showing off the skills of specially-bred black horses demonstrating a tradition that dates back to the fourteenth century.

The stunning neo-Gothic Town Hall building was opened in 1877 and is notable for its 85metre-high clock tower and intricate stone masonry details. There are also statues of prominent Mancunians along the façade at first floor level.

Manchester's Central Library is a relatively 'new' building. Its official opening was performed by King George V in 1934.

Opposite:
At Christmas the festive season starts with a spectacular firework display above the Town Hall...

...and colourful European markets fill the city's streets throughout December.

Chinatown emerged amongst once derelict Victorian warehouses.
The Imperial Chinese Archway that dominates the area was a gift to the
city from the Chinese people and is the only one in Europe.

Across the city, overlooking the Rochdale Canal, Canal Street is the focus of Manchester's Gay Village, one of the North West's most flamboyant nightlife destinations.

The Bridgewater Hall, one of the most acoustically
superior classical music venues in the world.

The University of Manchester is one of the largest in the United Kingdom.

The university is justly proud of its Whitworth Hall, a fitting venue for graduation ceremonies.

Thankfully, despite the over-protective health and safety concerns of the current times, graduates still choose to celebrate their hard-earned qualifications in the traditional manner.

The River Irwell is the natural boundary with the adjacent city, Salford.

Next stop Henley Regatta! The 'filing cabinet' building is the new Magistrates' Court.

The significance of the post box located beneath the glass bridge between Marks & Spencer and the Arndale Centre is revealed on the plaque attached to it.

(This post box remained standing almost undamaged on June 15 1996 when this area was devastated by a bomb. The box was removed during the rebuilding of the city centre and was returned to its original site on November 22nd 1999)